YUCATAN PENINSULA TRAVEL GUIDE FOR BEGINNERS

The Updated Concise Guide for Planning a Trip to Yucatan Peninsula Including Top Destinations,Culture,Outdoor Adventures,Dining,Cuisine and Getting Around

Nicolash Enzo
Copyright@2023

TABLE OF CONTENT

CHAPTER 1

INTRODUCTION

The state of Yucatán, located in northeastern Mexico on the Yucatán Peninsula, is a witness to the fusion of history, culture, and scenic beauty. With its wide variety of scenery, including beautiful beaches, lush forests, and historic ruins, Yucatán has established itself as a compelling location that draws tourists looking for an immersive experience that goes beyond typical travel. Let's explore the subtleties that make Yucatán unique, its historical importance, and the vibrant cultural tapestry as we travel virtually across this beautiful area.

Geographic Wonders and Importance

The geographic importance of Yucatán cannot be emphasized. The area, which is situated between the Caribbean Sea and the Gulf of Mexico, has a stunning coastline that spans for kilometers and provides sun-kissed beaches, clear seas, and a starting point for marine adventures. Visitors have access to the distinctive cenotes of the Yucatán Peninsula, which were created by the impact of a huge meteor millions of years ago and are a witness to the area's geological past.

Historical and Cultural Tapestry

Beyond its natural beauty, Yucatán's genuine fascination is found in its extensive cultural history. The Maya civilisation flourished in the area between the year 2000 BC and the sixteenth century AD, and its influence may still be seen today. Famous archeological sites like Chichén Itzá, Uxmal, and Tulum serve as reminders of the Maya people's sophisticated understanding of astronomy and architecture. These locations provide a look into a culture that had a keen awareness of the cosmos and created sophisticated systems for commerce, administration, and artistic expression.

The lifeblood of Mérida

Mérida, the capital, provides as a microcosm of the cultural diversity of Yucatán. Mérida epitomizes a seamless fusion of the past and present with its colonial-era architecture set beside thriving local markets and cutting-edge art venues. The city's big plazas, like the Plaza Grande in the center, are meeting places for both residents and visitors, and they often come alive with traditional dances, music, and festivals that reflect Yucatán's vibrant culture.

The enigma of Chichén Itzá

One of the New Seven Wonders of the World, Chichén Itzá, provides a window into the past. This historic city, home to magnificent buildings like the Kukulcán Pyramid, exemplifies the Maya people's mastery of mathematics and astronomy. The shadow of a snake is seen descending the steps of the pyramid during the spring and autumnal equinoxes, drawing tourists who are fascinated by the Maya culture's knowledge of astronomical phenomena.

Peace and quiet at Playa del Carmen

Traveling to Playa del Carmen's coastline attraction reveals another side to Yucatán's attractiveness. Water sports aficionados are drawn to the pristine beaches, clear seas, and vivid undersea environment. A variety of marine species may be seen when snorkeling and diving in the area's cenotes and at the Mesoamerican Barrier Reef, and the lively Quinta Avenida offers a wide selection of eating, shopping, and entertainment opportunities.

Where History Meets the Sea is Tulum.

The coastal ruins of Tulum provide a breath-taking view farther down the coast. These ruins, perched above cliffs overlooking the Caribbean Sea, provide an unmatched setting for getting in touch with the past. Travelers are invited to investigate the secrets of an old fortress city and then take in the splendor of the nearby beaches thanks to the site's historical importance and natural beauty.

Culinary Adventures and Cultural Immersion

Without connecting with its colorful culture and delectable food, one cannot properly experience Yucatán. Interacting with local groups opens access to traditional Mayan ways of life and crafts, giving one a better knowledge of the area's native heritage. Yucatecan cuisine, which combines Maya and European culinary traditions, tantalizes taste buds with dishes like cochinita pibil (slow-roasted pork) and papadzules (corn tortillas stuffed with pumpkin seed sauce).

Keeping the past alive while embracing the future.

Beyond its historical and cultural qualities, Yucatán is alluring. The area has shown a dedication to ethical and sustainable tourism, encouraging a respect for its native traditions and natural beauty. Local initiatives to save cenotes, encourage eco-friendly lodging, and interact with communities reflect a shared wish to keep Yucatán's character intact for future generations.

Last but not least, Yucatán entices visitors with its alluring fusion of history, culture, and natural beauty. The state symbolizes a story that spans millennia, from the intriguing remains of ancient civilizations to the vivid fabric of contemporary cities. The history of Yucatán is one of continuity, where the past and present coexist together, giving tourists the chance to fully immerse themselves in an experience that is both timeless and transformational. Yucatán offers a voyage that transcends the ordinary and embraces the remarkable, whether you are looking for historical marvels, tranquil beaches, cultural interactions, or a synthesis of all these components.

CHAPTER 2

Getting to Yucatán

The irresistible appeal of Yucatán's extensive historical background, stunning geographical features, and lively cultural heritage attracts tourists from many parts of the world. When considering the organization of your journey to the Yucatán region in Mexico, it is crucial to carefully navigate the many roads that lead to this destination. This first step is essential in preparing for the multitude of experiences that lie ahead. From the realm of aviation to the realm of local transportation, each stage of the voyage contributes an additional stratum of eager expectation and exhilaration.

Navigating airports and arrival points is a crucial aspect of air travel.

International passengers often start their trip to Yucatán through Manuel Crescencio Rejón International Airport, which is situated in the central region of Mérida, the capital city of the state. The contemporary airport has strong connectivity with several prominent cities around North America, making it a very handy point of entry. Upon disembarking, a profound sense of adventure permeates your being, a sentiment that is uniquely elicited by a location as multifaceted and captivating as Yucatán.

Cancún International Airport serves as a key gateway for those seeking to explore the Riviera Maya area. Located in the northeastern region of the Yucatán Peninsula, Cancún greets tourists with its vibrant ambiance and provides a diverse range of transportation alternatives to facilitate their forward exploration.

The Relationship Between Connecting Flights and Domestic Travel

Although there are direct flights to Mérida from many foreign locations, it is also possible to get connecting flights via major Mexican cities such as Mexico City and Cancún. These connecting flights not only give a convenient means of accessing Yucatán but also provide travelers the option to experience other areas of Mexico during their vacation.

For those who place importance on a varied travel encounter, the alternative of arriving in Cancún and embarking on an overland expedition to Yucatán offers an opportunity to see the shifting terrains, encompassing the azure seas of the coastline and the verdant foliage that typifies the interior of Yucatán.

Local Transportation in the Yucatán Region The present discourse aims to discuss the topic of local transportation within the Yucatán region.

Upon arriving in the region of Yucatán, the local transportation network efficiently and effectively facilitates the transfer of passengers to their desired locations. Various modes of transportation, including as public buses, taxis, and vehicle rentals, are easily accessible, accommodating diverse tastes and requirements.

Embracing the Public Transportation Experience: A Reflection on the Benefits and Advantages Public transportation has become an integral part of urban living, offering individuals a convenient and efficient means of commuting. This essay aims to explore the many benefits and advantages of

Public buses provide a cost-effective and genuine means of transportation around the area. The vibrant terminals serve as a representation of the diverse population of Yucatán, attracting both local residents and visitors from all backgrounds. As one starts a bus voyage, the scenic panoramas gradually unfurl beyond the window, offering fleeting views of rustic existence, time-honored remnants, and the dynamic communities that contribute to the fabric of the region.

Taxis: An Integration of Convenience and Comfort

Taxis provide a transportation option that is characterized by a higher degree of personalization, since they give direct routes to the desired location. In urban areas like as Mérida, there is a high abundance of taxis, which are often identifiable due to their vivid color schemes. Interacting with one's taxi driver has the potential to unveil valuable local knowledge and enrich one's trip experience. The act of pre-negotiating rates before to engaging in a transaction promotes a seamless and transparent process.

Car Rentals: Exploring at Your Own Speed

Car rentals provide those with a desire for independence in their journeys the opportunity to exercise autonomy by crafting their own travel plans. The presence of a well-maintained road network in Yucatán makes self-driving a feasible alternative. Exploring areas outside of the popular tourist destinations provides an opportunity to encounter hidden treasures, engage with the local community, and get insight into the distinctive characteristics that shape the essence of Yucatán.

Navigating Roadways and Observing Traffic Etiquette

Although the roads in Yucatán are typically well-maintained and easily traversable, it is important to possess knowledge of the local traffic regulations and customs. In urban areas, vehicular congestion may be dynamic, and the regulation of crossings often relies on implicit social norms. While traversing smaller towns and villages, one is met with a more leisurely tempo, affording the chance to fully grasp and admire the cadence of everyday existence.

The present section delves into the academic discourse around currency, payment, and practical considerations.

A comprehensive knowledge of local currencies and payment systems is necessary in order to provide a smooth travel experience. The designated legal tender in Mexico is the Mexican Peso (MXN), and it is recommended to possess a combination of physical money for minor transactions and electronic payment methods for substantial expenditures. Automated Teller Machines (ATMs) are conveniently accessible in urban centers, hence facilitating convenient and expeditious retrieval of financial resources.

Furthermore, possessing a fundamental understanding of the Spanish language may greatly augment one's ability to engage with local people, especially in less urbanized regions where skill in English may be restricted. The use of uncomplicated expressions and non-verbal actions of politeness significantly contribute to the establishment of interpersonal bonds and the exhibition of deference for indigenous traditions.

Embracing the Journey: Exploring Transportation Beyond its Utilitarian Function

In addition to the pragmatic considerations associated with reaching the destination of Yucatán, the voyage itself has significant importance within the context of the whole expedition. Regardless matter whether one is traversing the cerulean seas of the Caribbean or navigating through the verdant jungles, each passing instant prior to reaching the intended location is a chance to establish a profound connection with the fundamental nature of the Yucatán region.

The sense of anticipation upon arriving is reflected in the scenic vistas that gradually reveal themselves through the window, serving as a monument to the rich variety that characterizes Yucatán as a microcosm of the cultural and natural wonders found across Mexico. The act of traveling serves as a transitional phase that bridges the gap between the state of expectation and the subsequent realization. This process reaches its pinnacle with the revelation of the historical marvels, cultural abundance, and natural splendors that Yucatán has to offer.

In summary, the act of reaching Yucatán is not only a utilitarian endeavor, but rather an essential component of the immersive encounter that the region provides. The many means of transportation to Yucatán, including air travel, road trips, and local public transportation, provide opportunities for individuals to engage with the distinct landscapes, cultures, and customs that characterize this alluring location. As one embarks on the path of exploration, it is important to bear in mind that each step taken becomes a chapter within the Yucatán experience, contributing to the intricacy and liveliness of the tapestry of trip recollections.

CHAPTER 3

Destinations in Yucatán

The region of Yucatán, located in the northeastern part of the Yucatán Peninsula in Mexico, offers an intriguing combination of historical, cultural, and natural elements that attract tourists due to its varied array of attractions. The Yucatán area has a diverse range of sites that contribute to its magnetic attractiveness. These include the busy capital city of Mérida, the ancient archaeological marvels of Chichén Itzá, the picturesque seaside charm of Playa del Carmen, and the enigmatic ruins of Tulum. Together, these places provide a rich tapestry of experiences for visitors to explore.

Mérida: A Convergence of Past and Present

Located in the central region of Yucatán, Mérida serves as the vibrant capital city that epitomizes the fusion of historical legacy and contemporary dynamism. Mérida, renowned as the White City because to its many white-stone edifices, showcases a remarkable display of colonial architecture that serves as a tangible witness to its colonial heritage. The city's magnificence revolves on the renowned

Plaza Grande, a prominent plaza that pulsates with the vibrant cadences of local existence and festivities.

Mérida is a place that provides several opportunities for adventure. Embark on a leisurely stroll around the city's thoroughfares, where one may chance across concealed squares, elaborate places of worship, and bustling marketplaces that exhibit the indigenous artistry. The Paseo de Montejo, evocative of the renowned Champs-Élysées in Paris, showcases grand residences that evoke the historical period of Mérida's prosperity during the henequen boom. Art galleries, museums, and theaters provide valuable perspectives on the cultural abundance of Yucatán, while local markets showcase a vibrant array of colors and tastes. The cultural landscape of Mérida is enriched by the presence of traditional dances, music, and festivals, which serve to emphasize the city's dynamic and spirited atmosphere.

Chichén Itzá: An Insight into the Magnificence of Ancient Mayan Civilization

Chichén Itzá, designated as a UNESCO World Heritage Site and recognized as one of the New Seven Wonders of the World, is an archaeological phenomenon that provides insights into the sophisticated culture of the Maya. The aforementioned historical urban center, which was formerly a prosperous focal point for political, economic, and religious affairs, is most renowned for the Kukulcán Pyramid, sometimes referred to as El Castillo. The sophisticated architectural design of the pyramid is aligned with astronomical occurrences, resulting in the occurrence of the serpent's shadow during the equinoxes. This phenomena serves as evidence of the Maya civilization's remarkable understanding and mastery of astronomy.

In addition to the prominent pyramid, Chichén Itzá showcases a diverse range of architectural marvels. The Temple of the Warriors, the Great Ball Court, and the Observatory exemplify the profound comprehension of mathematics, astronomy, and engineering possessed by the Maya civilization. The provision of historical background and insights into the everyday lives of the Maya people is a key aspect of guided tours, which serve to enrich the overall experience.

Playa del Carmen, a coastal destination renowned for its scenic beauty and cultural amalgamation, offers a captivating experience for visitors.

Shifting our attention towards the coastal region, Playa del Carmen showcases an other aspect of Yucatán's captivating appeal. This coastal region, situated along the Caribbean Sea, emanates a relaxed atmosphere that attracts tourists in search of tranquility and water-based activities. The turquoise waves, fluffy white sand beaches, and coral reefs found at the playa provide an ideal environment for those who have an affinity for beaches and a passion for water-related activities.

The Quinta Avenida, also known as Fifth Avenue, serves as the energetic epicenter of Playa del Carmen, with a multitude of establishments such as stores, restaurants, bars, and captivating street art. As twilight descends, the town experiences a vibrant nocturnal ambiance, characterized by a diverse array of artistic expressions such as live musical performances, dance exhibitions, and cultural spectacles that pay homage to the cultural legacy of Mexico.

Tulum is a destination where the convergence of ancient ruins and unspoiled beaches takes place.

Located in the southern region of the coast, Tulum offers a compelling amalgamation of historical significance and picturesque landscapes. The Tulum archaeological site, situated on a precipice with commanding views of the Caribbean Sea, presents a captivating vista that captures the enigmatic essence of the Maya culture. The presence of temples and frescoes on the ancient remains of Tulum serves as evidence of the city's historical importance as a prominent port during the Maya civilization.

The appeal of Tulum goes beyond its archaeological site. The municipality's environmentally aware principles and artistic allure have garnered it recognition as a center for sustainable tourism. The presence of unspoiled coastlines accompanied by transparent bodies of water creates an inviting atmosphere for leisure and repose. Additionally, the existence of cenotes, which are naturally occurring sinkholes filled with freshwater, presents distinctive prospects for engaging in swimming and diving activities. In addition, the eco-friendly lodgings and health retreats in Tulum serve to provide a comprehensive and revitalizing holiday experience.

The topic of interest for this discussion is the concept of cultural immersion and its relationship to the exploration of culinary delights.

Although each site in Yucatán has its own unique characteristics, they combined provide immersive cultural experiences that enhance the overall vacation experience. The act of actively participating in local communities offers valuable perspectives on traditional Mayan traditions, handicrafts, and the routines of everyday life. Engaging in workshops and ceremonies gives guests the opportunity to establish significant connections and cultivate a more profound understanding of the indigenous heritage prevalent in the area.

The revelation of Yucatán's culture may be further facilitated via the pursuit of culinary discovery. The culinary tradition of the Yucatán region is characterized by the amalgamation of indigenous and European culinary influences, which culminate in a diverse and palatable assortment of gastronomic offerings. The culinary landscape of the area is characterized by many dishes, such as cochinita pibil, a pig delicacy that is slow-roasted, and sopa de lima, a soup infused with the tangy flavors of lime.

These gastronomic offerings serve as a testament to the historical and geographical influences that have shaped the local cuisine. Food markets, street sellers, and local cafes provide an opportunity to have a genuine culinary experience that is representative of the local culture and lifestyle.

The Appreciation of the Multiculturalism in Yucatán

In summary, the many places in Yucatán provide a wide range of experiences that respond to the diverse interests of every tourist. The city of Mérida showcases a unique combination of historical elements and contemporary features, while Chichén Itzá impresses visitors with its remarkable archaeological treasures. Playa del Carmen, on the other hand, entices tourists with its seaside charm and vibrant cultural fusion. Lastly, Tulum offers a captivating experience with its ancient ruins and emphasis on wellness. Together, these destinations collectively represent the diverse and varied personality of the Yucatán region.

As one traverses the many landscapes and interacts with the local populations, the intricate elements of Yucatán's cultural fabric converge, unveiling a territory that embodies a harmonious blend of enduring traditions and ongoing transformations. The many locations in Yucatán exemplify a state that appreciates its historical heritage while also inviting visitors to participate in its future. This exploration goes beyond mere tourism, capturing the very spirit of Yucatán's identity.

CHAPTER 4

Activities and Experiences in Yucatán

Yucatán, renowned for its rich cultural history, varied landscapes, and historical artifacts, offers a wide range of activities and experiences that respond to the varying interests of travelers. The Yucatán region offers a range of immersive experiences that allow individuals to interact with Mayan culture, explore cenotes, indulge in Yucatecan cuisine, and partake in nature and adventure activities. These opportunities provide travelers with the chance to deeply connect with the region's diverse offerings, creating lasting and impactful memories.

Exploring Mayan Culture: An Immersive Journey through History

Interacting with the indigenous culture of Yucatán is an opportunity to immerse oneself in a realm that is profoundly entrenched in historical and traditional foundations. The opportunity to visit local Mayan villages provides individuals with the possibility to engage with modern Maya culture, therefore facilitating a deeper understanding of historical customs and traditions. Under the guidance of community members, tourists have the opportunity to engage in workshops that provide instruction in traditional crafts, like weaving and ceramics. Additionally, they may actively participate in rituals that have been down through generations.

The exploration of Maya communities offers a unique chance to see the harmonious integration of traditional and contemporary elements. Engaging in dialogues with indigenous inhabitants provides valuable insights into their cultural practices, belief systems, and the obstacles they encounter in preserving their history. The process of acquiring knowledge about traditional herbal medicine and comprehending the cultural importance of ceremonies such as the Day of the Dead contributes to a profound recognition of the enduring strength and liveliness shown by indigenous populations throughout Mayan cultural immersion.

Title: Cenote Exploration: Enigmatic Subterranean Expeditions Cenote Exploration: Mystical Adventures Underground

The cenotes of Yucatán, which are natural sinkholes resulting from the collapse of cave systems, serve as a remarkable monument to the geological wonders found in the area. The Maya civilization has held great reverence for these underground bodies of freshwater for an extensive period of time. In the present day, these pools provide a unique opportunity for both investigation and recreational activities.

Engaging in snorkeling, diving, and swimming activities inside cenotes provides an opportunity to explore the concealed subterranean realm of the Yucatán region. The ethereal atmosphere is engendered by the interplay of light, whereby the sun's rays permeate the apertures in the cave's above, resulting in a captivating spectacle. Underwater caves, referred to as cenote caverns, provide divers the opportunity to explore fascinating rock formations and encounter distinct aquatic fauna. Every cenote has its own characteristics, with some ones being exposed to the open air, while others are situated beneath caverns, offering a diverse spectrum of experiences that span from tranquil reflection to thrilling escapades.

Title: Culinary Delights: An Exquisite Sensory Experience The title Culinary Delights: A Feast for the Senses has been revised to Culinary Delights: An Exquisite Sensory Experience to enhance its academic tone.

The culinary tradition of Yucatecan cuisine is characterized by its amalgamation of many gourmet elements, which serves as a testament to the cultural variety and historical influences that have shaped the region. The act of delving into the realm of gastronomy entails an investigation into the historical aspects, as it harmoniously amalgamates the authentic Mayan taste profiles with the European components that were added during the era of colonization.

Exploring renowned culinary creations like cochinita pibil, a delectable pig dish that through a lengthy roasting process and is seasoned in achiote, alongside papadzules, corn tortillas that are stuffed with a savory pumpkin seed sauce, presents an array of captivating sensory experiences. Street food sellers and local markets in Yucatán provide a diverse range of cuisines that effectively encapsulate the character of the region. A trip to a vibrant food market, such as the Mercado Lucas de Gálvez in

Mérida, offers an enthralling encounter where a fusion of colors, scents, and flavors harmoniously converge in a gastronomic symphony.

Nature and Adventure: Exploring the Abundance of Biodiversity

The region of Yucatán has a diverse array of natural landscapes, including verdant rainforests, unspoiled coasts, and well conserved biosphere reserves. This makes it an optimal choice for those who have a keen interest in nature and those who want thrilling experiences.

Engaging in the exploration of the biosphere reserves and national parks within the area provide individuals with many prospects for engaging in birding, animal observation, and trekking activities. The Ría Celestún Biosphere Reserve, renowned for its diverse avian population including flamingos, offers an opportunity for bird enthusiasts to see the brilliant pink flocks juxtaposed against the serene waters The Sian Ka'an Biosphere Reserve, designated as a UNESCO World Heritage Site, has a wide range of habitats, such as mangroves, lagoons, and coral reefs. The act of kayaking through the streams inside the reserve provides an opportunity to see and appreciate the complex interconnectedness of the many organisms that flourish within this protected environment.

Yucatán has a diverse range of possibilities for anyone in search of exhilarating and adrenaline-inducing experiences. The region's various landscapes provide an ideal setting for exhilarating adventures, ranging from ziplining through the rainforest canopy to going on ATV journeys over challenging terrains.

Responsible tourism, an approach that encompasses sustainability, is gaining prominence in the travel and hospitality industry.

The dedication of Yucatán to sustainable tourism is apparent via its efforts to safeguard its natural and cultural legacy. The act of participating in responsible travel practices is in accordance with the region's underlying principles of safeguarding its valuable assets for the benefit of forthcoming cohorts.

Tourists have the opportunity to endorse environmentally sustainable lodging options, actively engage in community-driven tourism programs, and adopt behaviors that mitigate their environmental footprint. Travelers make a significant contribution to the preservation of Yucatán's cultural diversity by demonstrating respect for indigenous customs and traditions.

The Personal Transformation of Experiences in Yucatán

In summary, the array of activities and experiences available in Yucatán extends beyond mere sightseeing, including valuable prospects for personal growth and development. The act of actively participating in the Maya society facilitates the development of cross-cultural comprehension and admiration. Exploring cenotes, natural sinkholes on the Yucatan Peninsula, encourages introspection and a sense of wonder. Embarking on culinary expeditions not only tantalizes the taste buds but also stimulates meaningful discussions. Engaging in nature and adventure activities allows individuals to reestablish a connection with the environment.

As one engages in the many activities offered in the region of Yucatán, they assume an active role in the narrative that is intricately crafted from the interplay of historical, cultural, and natural elements. Every encounter contributes to the expansion of one's comprehension of this intriguing area, imprinting a lasting impression on one's voyage and enhancing one's outlook on the interdependence of human existence and the global environment. The encounters in Yucatán extend beyond mere temporal occurrences, serving as conduits for deep relationships that beyond the confines of travel and echo deeply inside one's innermost being.

CHAPTER 5

Cultural Sensitivity and Responsible Travel in Yucatán

When embarking on a visit to the Yucatán area, which is renowned for its historical significance, cultural heritage, and stunning natural landscapes, it is imperative to prioritize the observance of cultural sensitivity and responsible travel practices. In addition to the captivating appeal of ancient marvels and breathtaking natural scenery, there exists a rich fabric of communities, cultures, and settings that warrant the highest degree of reverence and thoughtful contemplation. This discourse explores the importance of cultural sensitivity and responsible travel, its interconnectedness with the distinctive characteristics of Yucatán, and the strategies that visitors may use to establish a meaningful connection while promoting good outcomes in the destinations they explore.

Cultural Sensitivity: A Guiding Principle for Engaging with Communities

Cultural sensitivity is an integral facet of ethical travel, prioritizing the comprehension and reverence of the cultures, beliefs, and behaviors shown by the people encountered. The region of Yucatán, characterized by its rich indigenous history, places particular importance on the observance of cultural sensitivity. The Maya population, characterized by their extensive historical background and long-standing cultural practices, plays a fundamental role in shaping the identity of the area.

Effectively engaging with local communities requires a genuine disposition towards acquiring knowledge and actively listening. Prior to embarking on a journey, it is important to allocate sufficient time to do thorough study and acquaint oneself with the cultural customs and protocols prevalent in the region of Yucatán. This information enables those who are traveling to effectively manage social interactions in a manner that is considerate and polite, including many aspects such as greetings and gestures. By doing so, travelers are able to ensure that their presence in the destination is both pleasant and respectful, therefore making a valuable contribution.

The topic of discussion is to the need of showing reverence for sacred sites and traditions.

The region of Yucatán is characterized by the presence of many religious sites, remarkable archaeological structures, and locations of profound spiritual importance. When engaging in visits to such locations, it is essential to approach them with a sense of respect. Demonstrating adherence to established regulations, abstaining from physical contact or ascent on architectural elements, and complying with any limitations on photographic activities indicate a dedication to safeguarding the integrity and sacredness of these sites. The act of participating in the company of a knowledgeable local guide may provide valuable perspectives on the historical and spiritual backdrop, enhancing the whole encounter and promoting a sense of mutual regard.

Engaging in traditional rites and ceremonies provides a genuine insight into the cultural fabric of Yucatán. However, it is crucial to get consent and instruction from local people prior to participation. The act of observing rituals with humility and respect, while refraining from any kind of interruption or intrusion, is of utmost importance in order to properly acknowledge and pay tribute to their inherent value.

Language and communication play a pivotal role in establishing connections and fostering understanding among individuals and communities. By serving as a bridge, language facilitates the exchange of ideas, emotions, and information, enabling effective communication and promoting social cohesion. This essay explores the significance of

The use of language has significant importance in facilitating interpersonal interactions and exhibiting an awareness and respect for many cultures. In the region of Yucatán, a significant portion of the local population communicates in Spanish, particularly in metropolitan settings. Consequently, possessing a rudimentary grasp of Spanish expressions may significantly augment interpersonal exchanges. Utilizing Spanish greetings, expressing appreciation, and seeking permission to capture photographs in the native tongue may significantly contribute to the display of reverence for the indigenous culture.

Participating in dialogues with individuals from the local community, including craftsmen, sellers, and community members, offers a valuable avenue for acquiring knowledge about their cultural practices and attaining a deeper understanding of their unique viewpoints. The practice of active listening and the cultivation of open-mindedness are crucial in fostering meaningful dialogues that surpass linguistic boundaries and foster authentic relationships.

Responsible travel entails fostering a constructive influence.

Responsible travel encompasses not just cultural sensitivity, but also sustainable behaviors that prioritize the well-being of the environment, people, and local economy. In the territory of Yucatán, the interconnection between nature's valuable resources and the indigenous culture necessitates the adoption of responsible travel practices as a means of preserving the region's authenticity for the benefit of future generations.

The promotion of local economies and communities is a crucial aspect that warrants attention and support.

One of the most influential methods to provide assistance to local communities is by giving priority to local companies. The economic impact of tourists' decisions may be seen via several means, such as the direct procurement of goods from local craftsmen or the patronage of family-owned eateries. Participating in community-based tourism programs, which prioritize the direct economic benefits for local communities, facilitates the fair allocation of resources.

By selecting lodgings that promote sustainability and actively contribute to local efforts, tourists may effectively guarantee that their stay generates a beneficial impact. Eco-friendly hotels exemplify Yucatán's dedication to the preservation of its natural environment and indigenous cultural heritage.

The objective of this study is to explore strategies for reducing the environmental impact caused by human activities.

The preservation of Yucatán's distinct ecosystems, including cenotes and unspoiled beaches, is of utmost importance. Responsible travel encompasses the practice of minimizing one's environmental impact by ensuring the absence of any visible evidence of human presence, abstaining from causing any disruption to the natural habitats and behaviors of animals, and strictly following to prescribed routes and demarcated zones. It is important to exercise responsible conduct while participating in activities such as snorkeling and diving, in order to save marine species and ecosystems from any potential damage.

The region's environmental sustainability may be enhanced by the implementation of measures such as reducing plastic use, preserving water resources, and adopting responsible waste management practices. Engaging in beach clean-up projects, wherever feasible, serves to strengthen the dedication to conserving the pristine natural environment of Yucatán.

Educational Travel: Broadening Perspectives Traveling for educational purposes has shown to be a valuable means of expanding one's worldview and understanding of other cultures. By immersing oneself in unfamiliar environments, individuals

Responsible travel also encompasses the notion of imparting a lasting legacy of knowledge and awareness. Participating in educational travel endeavors, such as guided tours that prioritize cultural and historical backgrounds, facilitates the development of a more profound understanding of the given location. This comprehension, in return, instigates a feeling of need to safeguard and foster the locations and societies seen.

The topic of cultural exchange and empathy is of significant importance in academic discourse. This subject explores the dynamics of intercultural interactions and the development of empathy among individuals from different cultural backgrounds.

Responsible travel encourages people to actively participate in cultural exchange that goes beyond superficial encounters. Interacting with local people in a manner that transcends just economic exchanges facilitates a reciprocal process of knowledge acquisition and the cultivation of empathy. Engaging in a comprehensive comprehension of the difficulties, ambitions, and cultural practices of the people encountered throughout travel may result in a more profound and fulfilling travel experience, as well as a sustained sense of gratitude for the interpersonal bonds forged during the expedition.

In summary, the incorporation of cultural sensitivity and responsible travel is not only an auxiliary component of the travel experience, but rather an essential element thereof. The region of Yucatán, characterized by its rich indigenous history and varied landscapes, necessitates a mindful approach that prioritizes preservation, mutual respect, and constructive influence. As individuals engaged in the act of traveling, the decisions we make have a profound impact on the destinations we explore, resulting in a lasting influence that extends beyond mere physical imprints. This permanent legacy encompasses a rich fabric of comprehension, interconnection, and conservation, which significantly contributes to the intrinsic nature of Yucatán as well as the global community as a whole.

THE END

Printed in Great Britain
by Amazon

37124190R00030